W9-CFS-245

A
Special Gift

For:

Doris
_____
From:

Nancy
_____
Date:

Jan 11, 2000

Copyright © 1996
Brownlow Publishing Company
6309 Airport Freeway
Fort Worth, Texas 76117

All rights reserved.
The use or reprinting of
any part of this book
without permission of the
publisher is prohibited.

ISBN: 1-57051-123-3

Cover/interior:
Koechel Peterson & Associates

Printed in Singapore

Rose

Petals

Brownlow

Brownlow Publishing Company, Inc.

Little Treasures
Miniature Books

A Child's Tea Party

A Little Cup of Tea

All Things Great & Small

All Things Grow with Love

Angels of Friendship

Baby's First Book

Baby's First Book of Angels

Baby's First Little Bible

Dear Teacher

Faith

Faithful Friends

Flowers of Graduation

For My Secret Pal

From Friend to Friend

Grandmothers Are for Loving

Hope

Love

Mother

My Sister, My Friend

Precious Are the Promises

Quilted Hearts

Rose Petals

Soft as the Voice of an Angel

The Night the Angels Sang

'Tis Christmas Once Again

New Roses

The old dew still falls
on the old sweet flowers,
The old sun revives the
new fledged hours,
The old summer rears
the new-born roses.

ALGERNON CHARLES SWINBURNE

True friendship is no gourd, springing in a night and withering in a day.

CHARLOTTE BRONTË

If I Were a Rose

Oh, little rose tree, bloom!

Summer is nearly over.

The dahlias bleed,

and the phlox is seed.

Nothing's left of the clover.

And the path of the poppy

no one knows.

I would blossom if I were a rose.

EDNA ST. VINCENT MILLAY

Preparing for Roses

Preparing a bed for roses is a little like getting the house ready for the arrival of a difficult old lady, some biddy with aristocratic pretensions and persnickety tastes. Her stay is bound to be an ordeal, and you want to give her as little cause for complaint as possible.

MICHAEL POLLAN

Love every day.

Each one is so short

and they are so few.

NORMAN VINCENT PEALE

A rose is sweeter in the

bud than full-blown.

JOHN LYLY

I'd tiptoe

out to the back to see

whether I could catch

Grandfather in one of his

interminable conversations

with his flowers.

HELEN HAYES

A Little Flower

God, make my life

a little flower

That giveth joy to all;

Content to bloom

in native bower

Although its place be small.

MATILDA B. EDWARD

How Fair the Rose

How fair is the Rose!
What a beautiful flower.
The glory of April and May!
But the leaves are beginning to
fade in an hour,
And they wither and die
in a day.

Yet the Rose has one
powerful virtue to boast,
Above all the flowers of the field;
When its leaves are all dead,
and fine colors are lost,
Still how sweet a perfume
it will yield!

ISAAC WATTS

Beds of Roses

There should be *beds* of Roses,
banks of Roses, *bowers* of Roses,
hedges of Roses, *edgings* of Roses,
pillars of Roses, *arches* of Roses,
fountains of Roses, *baskets* of
Roses, vistas and *alleys* of the Rose.

DEAN HOLE

Flowers...have a mysterious and subtle influence upon the feelings, not unlike some strains of music. They relax the tenseness of the mind. They dissolve its rigor.

HENRY WARD BEECHER

Trust in the Lord and do good; dwell in the land and enjoy safe pasture.

PSALM 37:3

To analyze the charms of flowers is like dissecting music; it is one of those things which it is far better to enjoy than to attempt fully to understand.

TUCKERMAN

Roses

You love the roses—so do I.
I wish the sky would
rain down roses, as they rain
From off the shaken bush.
Why will it not?
Then all the valley
would be pink and white
And soft to tread on.
They would fall as light

*As feathers,
smelling sweet:
and it would be
Like sleeping and
yet waking,
all at once.*

GEORGE ELIOT

Be careful of little things. Life is a great bundle of little things.

OLIVER WENDELL HOLMES

Wild Rose

O wilding rose,

whom fancy thus endears,

I bid your blossoms

in my bonnet wave,

Emblem of hope and love

through future years.

SIR WALTER SCOTT

The Rosebush

If you dig a hole in the ground and put into it a Rosebush, filling one side of the hole with rich earth and the other with poor soil, every root of that Rosebush will leave the poor half to inhabit the rich and nourishing portion.

CELIA THAXTER

One of the worst mistakes
you can make as a gardener
is to think you're in charge.

JANET GILLESPIE

Earth with her thousand voices
praises God.

SAMUEL TAYLOR COLERIDGE

We blossom under praise
like flowers in sun and dew;
we open, we reach, we grow.

GERHARD E. FROST

Everywhere around the room
roses were sweeping into
depths of roses.

CANDACE WHEELER

God's gifts put man's best

dreams to shame.

ELIZABETH BARRETT BROWNING

Reign endless, Rose!

for fair your are, Nor heaven

reserves a fairer thing.

HERMAN MELVILLE

*My roses
are my jewels; the sun
and moon my clocks.*

LADY HESTER LUCY STANHOPE

*The cottage garden; most for
use designed, Yet not of
beauty destitute.*

CHARLOTTE SMITH

The wilderness
and the solitary
place shall be
glad for them;
and the desert shall
rejoice, and blossom
as the rose.

ISAIAH 35:1

Why Roses?

Perhaps few people have ever asked themselves why they admire a rose so much more than all other flowers. If they consider, they will find, first, that red is, in a delicately graduated state, the loveliest of all pure colors; and secondly, that

*in the rose there is no shadow,
except which is composed of
color. All its shadows are fuller
in color than its lights, owing to
the translucency and reflective
power of its leaves.*

JOHN RUSKIN

The best
rose-bush,
after all, is not that
which has the
fewest thorns but
that which bears
the finest roses.

HENRY VAN DYKE

Beautiful Rose

Beautiful Rose in
fragrance so rare,
Painted in colors bright,
Born of the sun and
pure gladsome air,
Fed by the dews of night.

J. H. KURZENKNABE

The Last Rose

'Tis the last rose of summer,
Left blooming alone;
All her lovely companions
Are faded and gone.

THOMAS MOORE

*W*ho reaches *with* a clumsy hand for a *rose* must not *complain* if the *thorns* scratch.

HEINRICH HEINE

No love, no friendship
can cross the path of our
destiny without leaving
some mark on it forever.

FRANÇOIS MAURIAC

Teach us delight
in simple things.

RUDYARD KIPLING

Two roses on one slender spray

In sweet communion grew,

Together hailed the morning ray

And drank the evening dew.

MONTGOMERY

A Day in the Sun

The serene philosophy of the pink rose is steadying. Its fragrant, delicate petals open fully and are ready to fall, without regret or disillusion, after only a day in the sun. It is so every summer. One can almost hear their pink, fragrant murmur as they settle down upon the grass: "Summer, summer, it will always be summer."

RACHEL PEDEN

Wake for shame,
my sluggish heart,
Wake, and gladly sing thy part:
Learn of birds, and springs,
and flowers,
How to use thy noble powers.

JOHN AUSTIN

Life is the flower of which
love is the honey.

VICTOR HUGO

The Roses
of Today

Live now, believe me,

wait not till tomorrow.

Gather the roses

of life today.

PIERRE DE RONSARD

*A flower unplucked
is but left to the falling,
And nothing is gained by not
gathering roses.*

ROBERT FROST

*God made the country,
and man made the town.*

WILLIAM COWPER

There is a garden in her face
Where roses and
white lilies grow.

ALLISON

Honor women! They entwine
and weave heavenly roses
in our earthly life.

JOHANN SCHILLER

The rose that with your

earthly eyes you see

Has flowered in God

from all eternity.

ANGELUS SILESIUS

Poor indeed is the garden

in which birds find

no homes.

ABRAM LINWOOD URBAN

Here's to friendship,
the only rose without thorns!

ANONYMOUS

What other planet
smells of roses?

PAM BROWN

A heart at peace
gives life to the body.

PROVERBS 14:30

The Tuscany Rose

The old, old black Tuscany Rose is the most precious rose of all. Mine came from an ancient garden that vanished long ago, but which used to be a glory to the town in which it grew. It is a hardy Rose also, in color so darkly red *as* to be almost black,—a warm *red*, less crimson than scarlet, *glowing* with a kind of smoul*d*ering splendor, with only two *rows* of petals round a centre of ric*h*est gold.

CELIA THAXTER

Sweet as Roses

Sweet as fragrant roses

'Tis to have a friend

On whom in gloom or sunshine

We know we can depend.

NINETEENTH-CENTURY
CALLING CARD

Garden
of Friendship

A friendship *can* weather
most things and thrive in thin
soil—but it needs *a* little mulch
of letters and phone calls and
small silly presents every
so often—just to save it from
drying out completely.

PAM BROWN

Love Planted a Rose

Love planted a rose,
And the world turned sweet,
Where the wheatfield blows,
Love planted a rose.
Up the mill-wheel's prose
Ran a music beat.
Love planted a rose,
And the world turned sweet.

KATHARINE LEE BATES

In the

depths of winter

I finally learned

that within me

there lay an

invincible summer.

ALBERT CAMUS

A

flowerless

room is

a soulless

room.

VITA
SACKVILLE-WEST

A friend is not only a rock of shelter to us in time of danger, but is also as rivers of water in a thirsty land, when our hearts cry out for life and love.

J. R. MILLER

*C*heerfulness is the atmosphere in which all things thrive.

JEAN PAUL RICHTER

A man who could make
one rose...would be
accounted most wonderful;
yet God scatters countless
such flowers around us!
His gifts are so infinite
that we do not see them.

MARTIN LUTHER

The rose

is sweetest wash'd

with morning dew,

And love is loveliest

when embalm'd

in tears.

Sir Walter Scott

A Rose Like You

A wild rose lives outside my door,
It asks no fost'ring care,
But grows in its appointed place
Because God put it there.
Each year in radiant June time
I welcome it anew,
For in its youth and joyousness
It is so much like you.

UNKNOWN

If We Would Have Roses

He who would have beautiful roses in his garden must have beautiful roses in his heart. He must love them well and always. He must have not only the glowing admiration, the enthusiasm, and the passion, but the tenderness, the thoughtfulness, the reverence, the watchfulness of love.

S. R. HOLE

It takes a long time

to grow an old friend.

JOHN LEONARD

O world, as God has made it!

All is beauty

ROBERT BROWNING

*W*ho loves a garden

loves a greenhouse too.

WILLIAM COWPER

A rose too often smelled

loses its fragrance

SPANISH PROVERB

*When at last
I took the time to look
into the heart of a flower,
it opened up a whole new
world…as if a window
had been opened to
let in the sun.*

PRINCESS GRACE
OF MONACO

*You can't forget a garden
When you have planted seed—
When you have watched
the weather
And know a rose's need.*

LOUISE DRISCOLL

Gardens are not made,

By singing—

"Oh, how beautiful!"

and sitting in the shade.

RUDYARD KIPLING

The vineyard of the LORD Almighty is the house of Israel, and the men of Judah are the garden of his delight.

ISAIAH 5:7

The Little Flower

This little flower, that loves the lea,

May well my simple emblem be;

It drinks heaven's dew as

blithe the rose

That in the King's

own garden grows.

SIR WALTER SCOTT

A Fondness for Roses

"I haven't much time to be fond of anything," says Sergeant Cuff. *"But when I have a moment's fondness to bestow, most times…the roses get it."*

WILKIE COLLINS

The Power to See

Grant me, O God,

the power to see

In every rose, eternity.

In every bud, the coming day;

In every snow, the promised May;

In every storm the legacy

Of rainbows smiling down at me!

VIRGINIA WUERFEL

We all know persons who are affected for better or for worse by certain odors.... Over and over again I have experienced the quieting influence of Rose scent upon a disturbed state of mind, feeling the troubled condition

smoothing out before I realized
that Roses were in the room,
or near at hand.

<small>Louise Beebe Wilder</small>

Who can behold the unfolding of each new spring and all its blossoms without feeling the renewal of "God's ancient rapture."

CELIA THAXTER

Over! the

sweet summer closes,

And never a flower at

the close; Over and gone

with the roses, And winter

again and the snows.

ALFRED, LORD TENNYSON

*Just living
is not enough....
One must have sunshine,
freedom and a little flower.*

HANS CHRISTIAN ANDERSEN